Dreamers and Doers

Darleen Ramos

Contents

Rigby®
A Harcourt Achieve Imprint

www.Rigby.com
1-800-531-5015

Introduction

Life is great, isn't it?

We have automobiles, trains, and aircraft that can take us wherever we want to go—even to outer space! Doctors have medicines and machines to make sick people well. Many diseases that were killing people a hundred years ago don't even exist today. We can watch movies in our homes with the push of a button, and we can even listen to music almost anywhere with the turn of a knob. And we have light! With just the flip of a switch we can light up homes, schools, and skyscrapers. We can use items made from plastic, rubber, paper, and all sorts of other things. We can do homework, play games, and keep in touch with almost anyone in the world with computers. We certainly do have everything we need, don't we? There couldn't possibly be anything else we need or want—all we have to do is sit back, relax, and enjoy all the things we have.

Well . . . what if people long ago thought that life was as good as it could be? What if they believed they had everything they needed? What if there weren't any scientists, dreamers, or doers? Would we still be surrounded by all the amazing machines, gadgets, and products that fill our lives today? Of course we wouldn't.

So come along! Let's meet a few of these scientists, dreamers, and people just like you, who weren't satisfied with the way things were, who wanted better things for themselves, their families, and their world, who weren't afraid to dream, and who did things to make their dreams come true.

Chapter 1

Maria Mitchell: "Question Everything"

(1818–1889)

When Maria Mitchell was born on August 1, 1818, on the quiet island of Nantucket, Massachusetts, no one could have predicted that she would study the stars and become a famous **astronomer.** During the 1800s, most girls in the United States would have been expected to learn only the things they needed to know to become wives and mothers. But Maria was not like most girls of her time—she loved books, mathematics, and sky gazing. Fortunately Maria's father believed that education was for everyone, and he encouraged her love for learning. Maria's father also shared with her his fascination with the night sky.

Maria Mitchell's love of astronomy inspired other young women to become scientists.

Mr. Mitchell was so interested in studying the night sky that he built his own **observatory** for looking at the stars on their rooftop, complete with a powerful telescope. He used this telescope to observe stars for the U.S. Coast Guard, and Maria often helped her father with this important work. The fishing crews and sailors of Nantucket, like most others in the world, used the stars to steer their ships. They relied on people like Maria and her father to provide the information and measurements they needed.

A telescope magnifies an object so the viewer can see things that the eye alone cannot see.

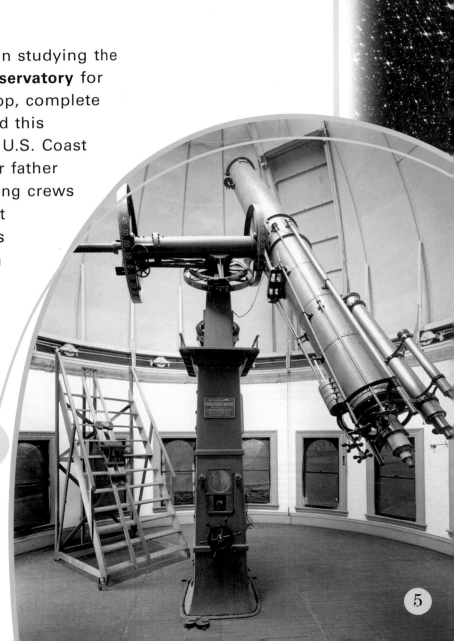

Maria attended school until she was 16, but she continued learning from her father and from professors and other teachers who often visited her family's home. Maria spent most days reading everything she could find and most nights observing the stars from her rooftop.

Then on October 1, 1847, something happened that would change Maria's life forever. She had gone to the rooftop to look through the telescope as usual, but she noticed something that she had never seen before—a faint, fuzzy light just above the North Star.

Studying the stars led Maria to an amazing discovery!

Some comets can be seen without a telescope, but others cannot.

She ran to tell her father about her discovery. They both thought that the object might be a comet, but they wanted to be sure.

Before they told anybody about the discovery, Maria and her father observed the object for several more nights, writing down its position each night. If the object moved from night to night, it was a comet. Imagine Maria's excitement when the object did indeed move!

Maria and her father shared their news with other scientists, and Maria was awarded a gold medal for being the first person to discover a comet that could only be seen with a telescope. Maria's discovery was named "Miss Mitchell's Comet."

This comet discovery made her famous, and she traveled all over the world meeting great scientists who were interested in learning more about this bright and curious young woman. The world was changing, and people were beginning to learn that women had a place in science.

A crater on the moon was named in honor of Maria Mitchell.

Maria returned to Massachusetts, and then continued her studies in New York at Vassar College, a school for women, where she later became the first female astronomy professor in the United States. Maria Mitchell was a wonderful teacher, and her students loved her because she believed in them. To Maria, her greatest accomplishment was sharing her love of science and astronomy with a new generation of women. She encouraged her students to make their own amazing discoveries by telling them, "We especially need imagination in science. . . . Question everything!"

It was at Vassar College that Maria Mitchell became the first female teacher of astronomy in the United States.

Chapter 2

Carlos J. Finlay:
The Mosquito Man

(1833–1915)

Like Maria Mitchell, Carlos J. Finlay had a curious mind and a love of learning. Also like Maria, Carlos Finlay wasn't satisfied with how things were—he wanted to make things better.

Born on December 3, 1833, in Cuba, Carlos J. Finlay was raised on a coffee farm owned by his father, who was a doctor. Instead of going to school, Carlos was taught at home by an aunt. At the age of 11, Carlos was sent to attend school in France.

Carlos J. Finlay became a doctor, like his father.

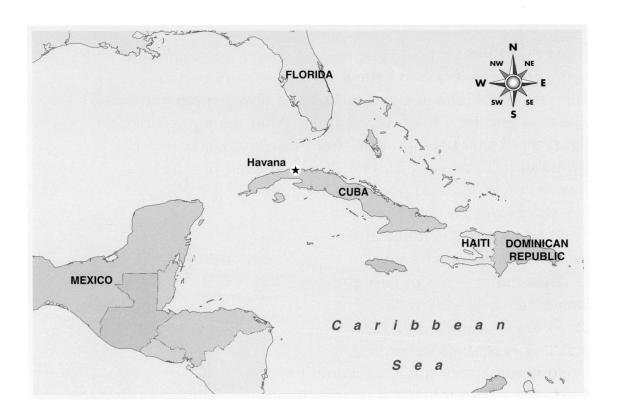

When he was 18, Carlos began studying to become a doctor at Jefferson Medical College in Philadelphia, Pennsylvania. After he finished his studies, Carlos spent several years studying in Europe. When it was time for him to return to Cuba, a good friend gave him a microscope. Now a doctor, Carlos Finlay was ready to care for the sick of Havana, Cuba.

At that time in the 1860s, many Cubans were suffering and dying from cholera and yellow fever, two very serious illnesses. Dr. Finlay wanted to find out how people got these diseases and how they were spread. After much research, he figured out that cholera came from drinking water that had **germs** in it. Though much later it was proved that he was correct, most medical people at the time did not accept Finlay's **theory**. And they found his ideas about yellow fever even stranger!

After many years of caring for people with yellow fever, Dr. Finlay announced in 1881 that this fever was spread by mosquitoes. Today this idea would be accepted, but in the 1880s, many people believed that diseases could only be spread from person to person. The idea of an insect spreading such a terrible disease was so ridiculous to most people that they made fun of Dr. Finlay, calling him "The Mosquito Man."

There are several serious diseases that can be caused by mosquito bites.

Why "Yellow Fever"?

Yellow fever is an often deadly disease found mainly in damp, hot areas of the Americas and Africa. It causes a high fever, body aches, vomiting, and liver and kidney damage. It gets its name from the yellow skin and eyes that people develop when they are infected with the disease.

Many yellow fever patients died from the disease, not only in Cuba, but also in the United States, where yellow fever killed many people in Philadelphia and New Orleans.

13

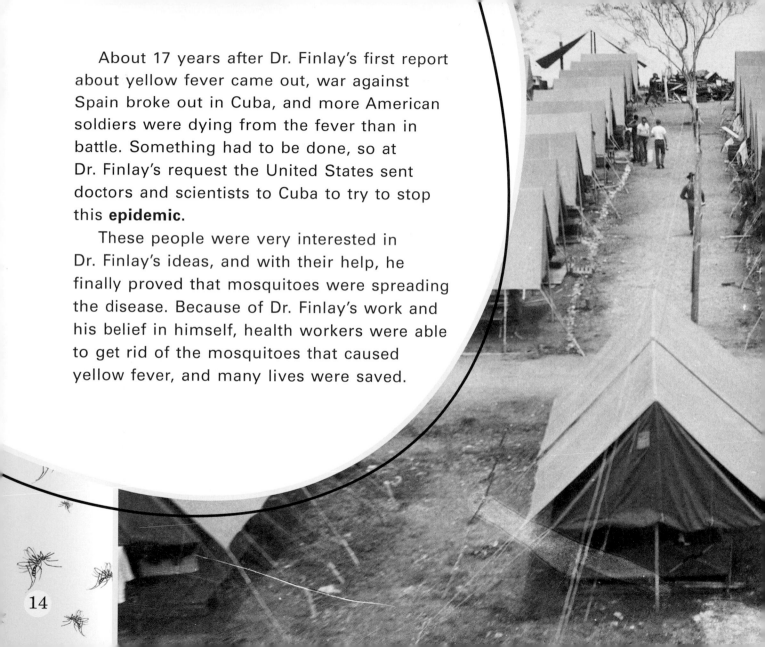

About 17 years after Dr. Finlay's first report about yellow fever came out, war against Spain broke out in Cuba, and more American soldiers were dying from the fever than in battle. Something had to be done, so at Dr. Finlay's request the United States sent doctors and scientists to Cuba to try to stop this **epidemic**.

These people were very interested in Dr. Finlay's ideas, and with their help, he finally proved that mosquitoes were spreading the disease. Because of Dr. Finlay's work and his belief in himself, health workers were able to get rid of the mosquitoes that caused yellow fever, and many lives were saved.

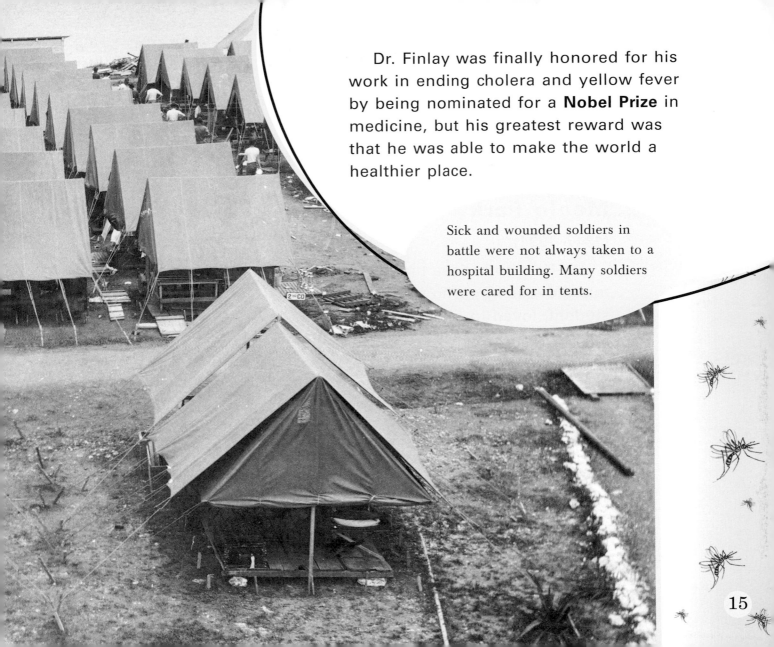

Dr. Finlay was finally honored for his work in ending cholera and yellow fever by being nominated for a **Nobel Prize** in medicine, but his greatest reward was that he was able to make the world a healthier place.

Sick and wounded soldiers in battle were not always taken to a hospital building. Many soldiers were cared for in tents.

15

Chapter 3

Thomas Alva Edison: The Wizard of Menlo Park

(1847–1931)

It's hard to believe that a mischievous boy who was a poor student, loved to play practical jokes, and was nearly deaf would grow up to be one of the most famous scientists and inventors the world has ever known. But that's the story of Thomas Alva Edison.

Thomas Edison began experimenting in his basement when he was just a child. He could not have known that he was on his way to becoming a great inventor.

Thomas Edison was born on February 11, 1847, the seventh and youngest child of Samuel and Nancy Edison in Milan, Ohio. His early teachers called him "addled" (which means confused) and a slow learner. This made his mother so angry that she took Thomas out of school and decided she would teach him at home. It was actually good for the naturally curious boy to learn one-on-one, and it helped Thomas concentrate on what he liked best— scientific inventions.

Thomas Edison was born in this house.

When he was 15, Thomas rescued the young son of a telegraph operator from getting crushed by a train. As a reward, Thomas was given telegraph lessons and a job as an operator. This job led Edison to develop improvements in the telegraph. He not only discovered a way to send images over telegraph lines, but he also designed a faster telegraph that could send four messages on a single wire instead of just one.

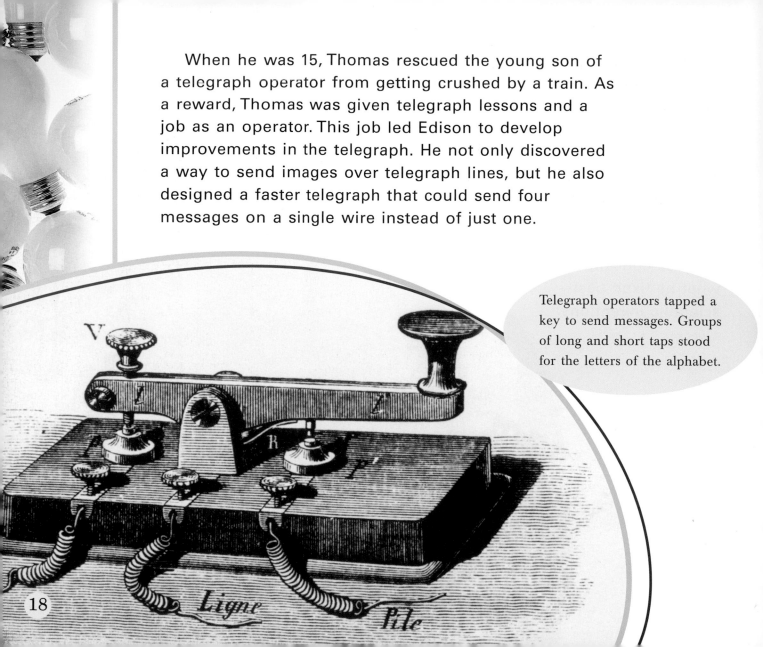

Telegraph operators tapped a key to send messages. Groups of long and short taps stood for the letters of the alphabet.

Thomas Edison's work on the telegraph caused people to notice this bright young man and his very bright ideas. But Thomas was just getting started! In 1876 he built a **laboratory** for his experiments that was known as the "invention factory" in Menlo Park, New Jersey. Thomas Edison was constantly thinking of new inventions and better ways of doing things. He worked long hours and expected those around him to do the same. He once said, "There's no substitute for hard work," meaning that accomplishments come only with hard work.

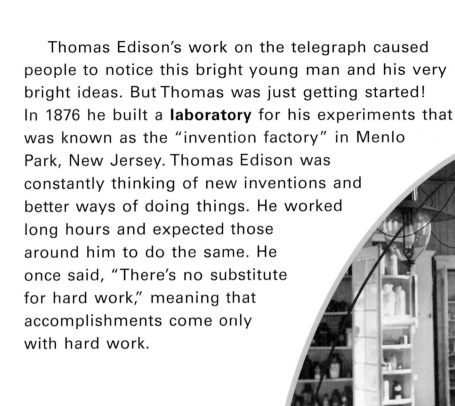

Edison's "invention factory" included science laboratories, machine and pattern shops, a library, and rooms for experiments.

In Thomas Edison's 84 years, he invented hundreds of gadgets and devices. Among his inventions are the phonograph, a talking doll, an electric pen, and the kinetograph, the first easy-to-use motion-picture camera. The kinetograph didn't make the kind of movies you watch today, but it was the beginning of the thrilling wide-screen entertainment we all now enjoy.

Does Edison's phonograph look anything like your CD player?

People used a kinetoscope—a machine like this—to watch the short movies made by a kinetograph. A person would look through the hole on top as a strip of film moved in a circle inside, with a bright light flashing quickly behind each picture so that the pictures themselves seemed to be moving.

Some of Edison's Best-Known Inventions

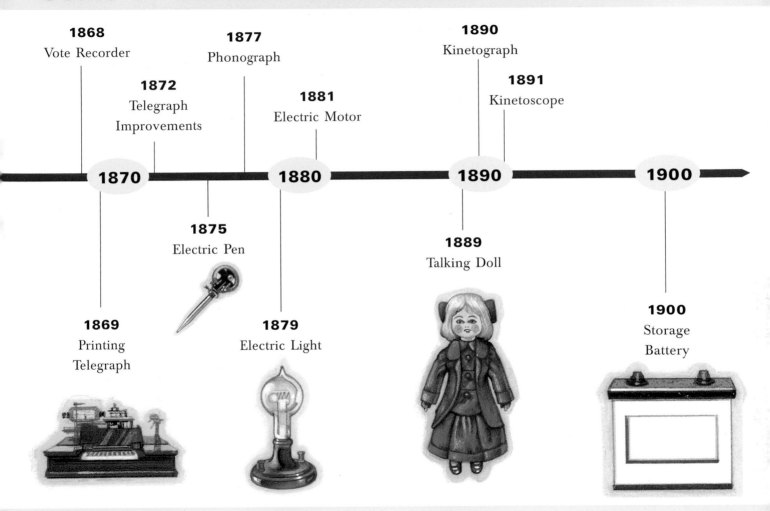

1868
Vote Recorder

1872
Telegraph
Improvements

1877
Phonograph

1881
Electric Motor

1890
Kinetograph

1891
Kinetoscope

1870

1880

1890

1900

1875
Electric Pen

1889
Talking Doll

1869
Printing
Telegraph

1879
Electric Light

1900
Storage
Battery

Though Thomas Edison invented many things that changed the way people live, he is probably most remembered for his work on the lightbulb. Edison didn't actually invent the lightbulb (many scientists throughout the world were working on this invention at the same time), but he did invent a long-lasting bulb that would be usable in homes and businesses. And then because there were few places that had electricity, Edison invented an electric power system that made electricity available to everyone. It can honestly be said that Thomas Edison lit up our lives!

Thomas Edison received many awards and honors during his lifetime, but the most fitting one occurred on October 21, 1931, the evening of his funeral, when President Herbert Hoover requested that all electric lights be dimmed in the White House as well as in homes and businesses throughout the world. What a perfect tribute to the man who had brought light to so many.

The unusual materials Edison used while trying to create a long-lasting lightbulb included bamboo and cotton. This one uses a special cotton thread.

22

The streets of New York City were lit with gas lamps before electricity became widely available.

Chapter 4

George Washington Carver: The Plant Doctor

(about 1865–1943)

When you think of peanuts, what comes to mind? Peanut butter and jelly sandwiches for lunch? Eating peanuts from the shells at ball games? Peanut oil shampoo? Maybe you've never heard the last one, but that doesn't mean there's no such thing as shampoo made from peanuts.

George Washington Carver discovered hundreds of uses for common plants.

In fact, George Washington Carver, a famous American scientist and educator, developed shampoo as well as more than 300 other useful products from peanuts in order to help the American farmers.

Cheese, sandwiches, soap, glue, and medicine are only a few ways to use peanuts.

George was born the son of a slave mother on the Moses Carver plantation in Missouri near the end of the American Civil War. Though the exact date of his birth is unknown, it was probably sometime in the spring of 1865. George and his mother were kidnapped by night riders when George was still an infant. Moses Carver was able to get George back, but unfortunately his mother was never seen or heard from again.

The Carvers raised George and his brother Jim as their own sons. The Carvers realized that George was a gifted and intelligent child and encouraged him to learn all that he could.

Due to childhood illnesses, George wasn't able to work in the fields on the plantation, so he helped with inside chores instead. This left him plenty of free time to walk through the nearby woods learning all he could about the different plants growing there.

Even as a child, George was interested in the many kinds of plants that grew near his home.

Eventually George learned so much about plants that the Carvers and people from nearby farms would come to him with all their plant questions. George didn't disappoint them. He usually had the answers! This earned him the nickname "the plant doctor."

In 1896 Carver came to the Tuskegee Institute as a teacher.

By the time he was 12 or 13, George had learned all he could from the Carvers and from the all-black school he attended in a nearby town. It was time for him to move on and get the education he wanted. George did graduate from high school and later became the first African American student to attend Iowa State College. When he finished college, George began teaching at Iowa State College and later taught at the Tuskegee Institute in Alabama.

George's arrival in Alabama couldn't have come at a better time. For years cotton was the biggest cash crop in the South, but unfortunately, growing cotton year after year took minerals out of southern soil. If the cotton crop was poor, the farmers were left with nothing to sell, and they certainly couldn't eat cotton! And as if things couldn't get any worse, the boll weevil, an insect that destroys fields of cotton, was invading the South. Things were not good for cotton farmers until George decided to try to help them.

Boll weevils destroyed cotton crops.

George thought the best solution was for the farmers to grow other cash crops like sweet potatoes, pecans, and peanuts, but most farmers didn't think anyone would buy these crops. So George went one step further. He developed 75 different products from pecans, 118 from sweet potatoes, and over 300 from peanuts!

Though George Washington Carver is best known for all the things he developed from peanuts—plastic, milk, hand lotion, and cooking oil, to name a few—he was more than just a scientist. His most important role was as a teacher. He taught his students and others to look beyond what is right in front of them. He dared them to discover what they might have missed at first glance.

Paste, paint, and cloth are only a few of the products that George Washington Carver made from sweet potatoes.

Examples of Plant Products
Developed by George Washington Carver

Plant	Food	Health and Beauty	Household Products	Other
Peanuts	peanut butter pancake flour vinegar coffee candy milk margarine cooking oil chili sauce mayonnaise cheese peanut sausage pickles soup punch	hand lotion face cream shampoo shaving cream soap face powder baby cream medicines	laundry soap glue shoe polish paper	dyes for clothes leather dyes paints printers' ink charcoal wallboards linoleum (floor covering)
Sweet Potatoes	flour vinegar coffee candy sugar chocolate	medicines	paste shoe polish ink paper	dyes paints cloth rubber

Chapter 5

An Wang:
A Generous Genius
(1920–1990)

In the 1960s, computers were larger than cars, and **calculators** were as big as TV sets—certainly nothing you'd want to carry around! Now you can carry a calculator in your pocket and a computer in your backpack. And you can thank a man named An Wang for these improvements.

An Wang made calculators and computers easier for ordinary people to own and use.

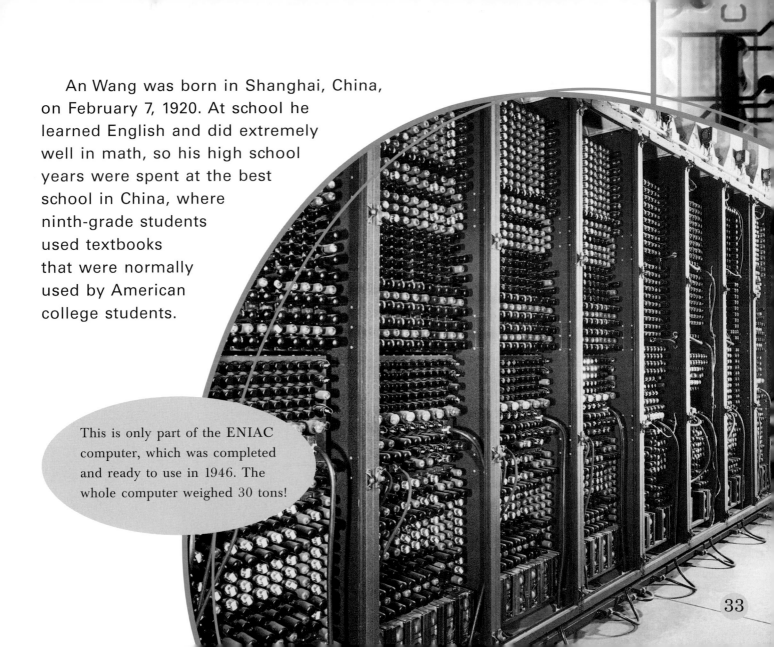

An Wang was born in Shanghai, China, on February 7, 1920. At school he learned English and did extremely well in math, so his high school years were spent at the best school in China, where ninth-grade students used textbooks that were normally used by American college students.

This is only part of the ENIAC computer, which was completed and ready to use in 1946. The whole computer weighed 30 tons!

An then went to college in Shanghai, and after he graduated, he helped teach classes at the university. But An and others had to leave the country because Japan was about to invade China. The rest of his family wasn't able to get out of Shanghai before the attack, and several of his relatives were killed, including his sister. While he was away, An learned about and applied for a program that would train scientists in the United States to help rebuild China after the invasion.

After the Japanese invaded Shanghai during World War II, college students like An Wang were moved to a safer place.

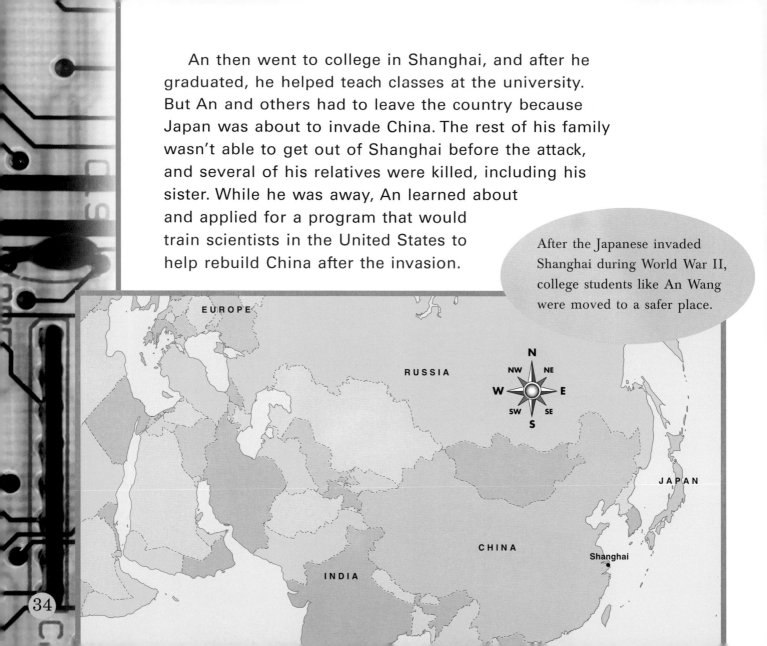

EUROPE

RUSSIA

N
NW   NE
W   E
SW   SE
S

JAPAN

CHINA

Shanghai

INDIA

In 1945 An moved to Virginia, in the United States. He was still thirsty for knowledge and returned to college at Harvard University in Boston, Massachusetts. After he graduated, he started working in the computer lab at Harvard, where he invented a way to store memory in a calculator by using magnets! This invention was only the beginning for An Wang. This creative **genius** was just getting started.

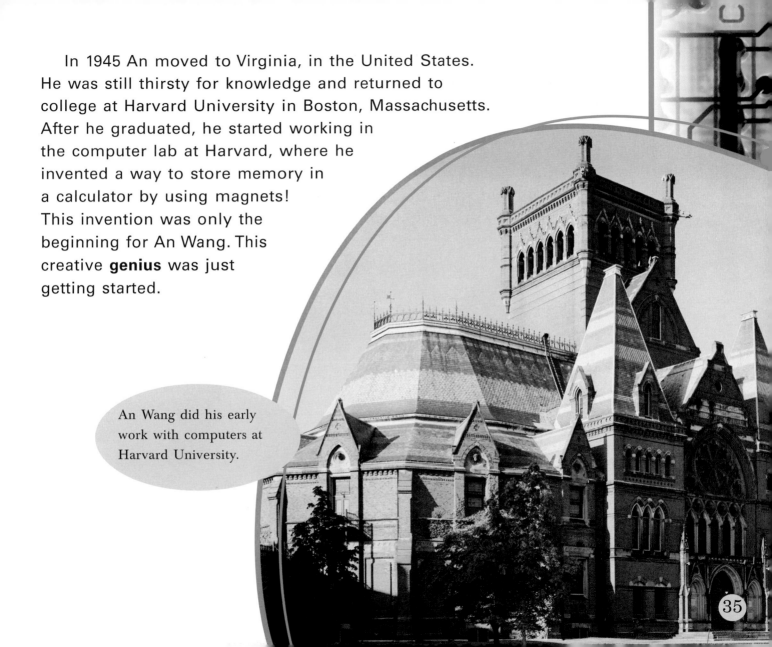

An Wang did his early work with computers at Harvard University.

With only $600, he began Wang Laboratories and worked to improve the calculator. Because of Wang's work the calculator could compute more sets of numbers in a shorter period of time than ever before. People bought these improved calculators because they weren't expensive. Now An wanted another challenge, so he started working on **word processors** and small computers. Wang Laboratories grew and became a very successful company.

Largely because of An Wang's work, calculators and computers have been greatly improved.

The first calculators were not small and did not compute very fast.

An Wang was generous with his time and his money. He gave millions of dollars to the city of Boston, Massachusetts, to restore their performing arts center and to build a new section at one of the larger city hospitals. He also donated one million dollars to Harvard University to support Chinese studies. An Wang used his intelligence and scientific mind to help many people, either through his inventions or through his generosity.

The Metropolitan Theatre was beautiful when it opened in 1925, but by 1983 it needed major repairs. When An Wang made his generous donation, the center was renamed The Wang Center for the Performing Arts.

The Power of Invention

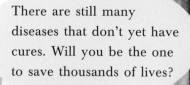

Sally Ride was the first American woman to travel in space. No doubt Maria Mitchell would be proud.

The inventors and scientists in this book were definitely dreamers, but they also wanted to know how things worked, and they wanted to solve problems. Their creative ideas and scientific discoveries have helped and inspired people all around the world!

Wouldn't they be pleased that their curiosity and determination encouraged others to travel into outer space and to find cures for deadly diseases? Wouldn't they be happy that their discoveries made life easier and more healthful for millions of people? Yet there is still much to do—and it can begin with you! Young minds must keep dreaming of better ways to do things—whether it's a new cure for a disease or a new way to use plastic. So start dreaming—and then get out there and do it!

There are still many diseases that don't yet have cures. Will you be the one to save thousands of lives?

Glossary

astronomer a scientist who studies stars, planets, suns, moons, and other objects in space

calculator a device that can do math

epidemic the rapid spreading of a disease making many people sick at the same time

genius a person with very great mental skill and ability

germ a very tiny living thing that causes disease

laboratory a place for doing scientific experiments or for creating or testing new products

Nobel Prize a special prize given every year to people who have made important contributions to science, medicine, peace, literature, and economics

observatory a building or room with telescopes used to view the stars and other objects in space

theory an idea that explains how or why something happens, but that has not been proved

word processor a computer-like machine that can be used to type, edit, and print letters and papers

Index